The Way It Is

This book has the unique capability to access a video of the picture displayed by inserting the link on YOUTUBE or GOOGLE. Once on the internet, additional related videos are automatically available for your reading pleasure.

The Way It Is

A BOOK OF FICTION BASED ON FACT

...

Ruth DiDomenico

GRAPHICS BY DOMINIC DIDOMENICO

ISBN: 1517459788
ISBN 13: 9781517459789
Library of Congress Control Number: 2015915641
CreateSpace Independent Publishing Platform
North Charleston, South Carolina

Acknowledgments

• • •

FIRST I WANT TO THANK our grandchildren Dominic DiDomenico and Kelly Tarantola for their time and superior computer skills for meshing the script with the pictures that describe the story, and our sons Steve and Eric DiDomenico for helping in this effort.

Thanks to Chris Jordan, photographic artist, for permission to use images from his remarkable film on Midway Island.

David Schreiner (Lt. Col., US Army, retired) and Dr. Sue Ann Cairns have edited this script and made significant contributions to every portion of this book, and their assistance is much appreciated.

A hearty thanks to Joyce Scales for her help with assembly of material and many hours of coordination with the publisher.

Also, I want to thank the Writers Group at Laurel Manor in the Villages, Florida, for their enthusiastic support, encouragement, and suggestions for this project.

Ruth L. DiDomenico

Table of Contents

Introduction

• • •

THE FOLLOWING BOOK IS FICTION, but it is based on scientific fact gleaned from on-site research by many people over many years at Midway Island Atoll. I was privileged to spend two weeks in 1997 as a part of this site's research study with the Elderhostel (now Road Scholars), directed by the National Oceanic and Atmospheric Association.

The islands of Midway Atoll are located in the middle of the Pacific Ocean, northwest of Hawaii and halfway to Japan. Midway is also the major breeding ground of the spinner dolphins and many species of birds, including approximately 85 percent of the world's Laysan albatrosses and 45 percent of the world's black-footed albatrosses. The two species of albatross do not mix, as their movements are different and the mating dance of each is not pleasing to the other.

Occasionally there is an attack by excited juveniles, resulting in a mixed chick with both characteristics. The following story is of the cause and effect of just such a circumstance. I have chosen to give the main character's names and the ability to speak as we know it in order to illustrate the facts.

There is no food on the island, so it is imperative that a chick be ready to fly, or else it will die. The parent will withdraw and leave the chick to its fate. Ten percent of these chicks drown, while others are eaten by the sharks that wait by the dozen for just such a meal. At this point it is heartbreak or glory for all.

CHAPTER 1
The Hook

• • •

https://youtu.be/AxRtMk5pyQ4

HE FELT THE JERK BEFORE he felt the pain. His body followed a downward plunge into the icy waters. He pulled his head backward to escape his snare and again felt the sharp pain in his beak. He flapped his wings and twisted his body back and forth, but the gaping hole in his beak became larger and the pain was now unbearable. Vinnie could feel the water flowing through the hole in his beak and his head being dragged under water. He struggled for air, but his lungs filled with water, and pain was the last thing he remembered.

A barge was making its way slowly across the sea. It was being towed by a tug less than one-tenth its size. As was the custom, the barge crew laid out a long line with baited hooks attached about every one hundred feet to catch fresh fish for their meals. The bait looked appetizing to any passing sea creature. As a result of this lure, many were hooked, pulled under, and killed. To most bargemen, drowned sea birds were not the intended target and were a waste of good bait.

A lone man standing on the barge had watched Vinnie dive after the bait and get caught on one of the long line of hooks being dragged behind the barge.

"Dang," said the man. "Another one of them stupid birds has snatched my bait again." He walked a few steps and called to a second man who was tending some lines on the other side of the barge.

"Nick, are you busy? Come over here and help me unload this line before this stupid bird breaks it. Sure is hard to make a decent catch any more with all the pests flying around and stealing our bait."

Nick secured the line he was working on and walked over to the end of the barge. He looked out and saw the white blob about two feet under the water on the third hook. He leaned over and began the hand-over-hand pull of the fishing line.

"Look what we have here," said Nick. "We got ourselves a salmon on hook two." Ned took the fish off the hook and placed it in a bucket near the corner of the end support. He continued to pull.

"Do you suppose that we ought to shorten the length between the hooks? This sure gets to be a lot of work. Maybe we ought to bait each twenty-five feet instead of fifty to a hundred feet," replied Ned.

"This one is a big fellow. Maybe we ought to get the net to lift him out before he breaks our hook," said Nick. Ned reached over and picked up the net that was nestled in a holder on the rail. Ned cupped Vinnie in his net and then in a quick movement tossed him over his shoulder onto the deck.

Vinnie landed with a thud.

"Let's be sure we get that hook back from that bird. We are running short of hooks, and we have a long way to go." Ned nodded in agreement. He knelt down near Vinnie to take the hook from his beak. The eyes of the bird were now open and watching him. When Ned reached out to touch Vinnie, he lifted his head and spread his wings. Vinnie's breath was coming fast and shallow. His heart was beating fast. His eyes were darting, looking for an escape. He got on his feet and backed up, but the hook kept him from moving.

Ned sat on his heels and looked at Vinnie. He saw a magnificent animal with spirit, a giant of a bird whose entire body was pure white from his pink torn beak to his pink webbed feet. His tail was sooty brown, and his wings lined mostly with white feathers with black edges. .

Nick said, "You are taking a long time. Come on and help me get this salmon off line six. We are going to have a feast this evening."

Ned ignored Nick and slowly put his hand out toward Vinnie, who smelled the oil, smoke, and fish on the human. The deck was hot on his feet, and he stepped from one foot to the other, trying to get as far away from this human as he could. Any movement increased the pain. Vinnie was at the end of the line pulling on his beak.

Nick reached out slowly and put one hand behind Vinnie's head. With the other he gently lifted the hook from Vinnie's beak. It was an easy task to lift the forked hook through the gaping hole. He leaned back on his heels and stood up, giving Vinnie more room.

Vinnie winced as the man touched his head. He had never been touched by a human before. He felt relief from the drag of hook and line, but his heart was pounding from pain and fear and uncertainty.

Nick looked over and saw bird and man staring at each other, neither making a move. He finished rolling up the line and stood with his hands on his hips. Ned was holding out his hand to Vinnie, and Vinnie was edging closer to the outstretched hand.

Nick said, "You have been on the ocean too long, Ned; looks to me like you are getting soft in the head. If I didn't know better, I would think you are falling in love."

Ned looked up and pulled his hand away. "I can't be had that easily," he said. "Don't ever let it be said that Ned Bolton can be had with one soulful look, but it wouldn't hurt to feed this bird some gruel. He won't be able to catch much on his own for a while with that beak."

Nick moved forward to smash Vinnie with his boot, saying, "I think we ought to kick him in the head and put him out of his misery."

Ned stood up and blocked Nick from reaching Vinnie. "Leave him to me. I will just feed him some scraps, and it might be amusing to have some company. I get tired of looking at your ugly face all of the time. This one is so much prettier."

Nick backed off and looked at his friend. "OK for now, but if I find any fleas in my bed, I am going to shoot him and probably wound you." He picked up the bucket with three salmon in it and headed for the galley.

Ned turned around and looked at Vinnie. He knew that the bird would not understand him, but said anyway, "You wait here; I will find something for you to eat."

He turned and walked toward the galley. When he came back with some fish heads and entrails, Vinnie was gone.

CHAPTER 2

The Restless Feeling

• • •

VINNIE STOOD ON THE DECK alone. He stepped forward to find that his legs were unsteady. He spread his wings and could feel the wind through his feathers, but it was as if his wings were being pushed up rather than lifted. He could still feel the touch of the human on his body and shuddered in revulsion. He looked out at the sea behind him and wanted to leave this place of pain.

He took a few halting steps and lifted his wings. He took several running steps. When his feet no longer touched the deck, he was in the air. Soon exhausted, he landed on the water and waited for fish to appear. He was too weary to search for food.

Vinnie was shaken, and very aware of the damage to his beak. He dipped it in the cool water and let it remain there for a short time. This seemed to make the pain less severe. Special glands below the eyes of the albatross remove excess salt when it drinks seawater. The salty waste liquid produced by the glands then comes out of the nostrils from this tube, runs down the grooves in the bill, and drips off the end of the beak. He tried to force the salty liquid through the tube, but it would not flow out of his left tube. There was a great pain, making him anxious and restless. It is life threatening for an albatross, or any wild thing, to lose body functions.

Later that evening, a small squid swam toward him. He reached out and plucked it from the water.

The plucking was painful, but the swallowing was good. He searched for others until he was full. He rested on the water until the sun came over the horizon.

Deep inside there was a hunger for something he could not identify. The hunger would not go away, yet the sea was now practically brimming with tasty morsels of squid and fish eggs. He longed for something—what? He remembered the joy of flying, buoyed by the wind.

He began to move his big webbed feet in the water. Soon he was running, and his wings beat vigorously. In a few short beats Vinnie was in the air. He wanted to fly far away from this empty place of pain. He played in the air currents that pushed him without effort. Part of his brain rested, while the other part was alert for danger or direction. He flew for many hours seeing nothing but sky and water. Still this strange restless feeling followed him. He flew down toward the surface, spread his tail, dragged his big webbed feet, and then landed on the water. He wanted to understand this unrest.

He closed his eyes briefly, threw his head back and to the side, and let out a cheerful howl for all the world to hear. He floated on the water for a long while and yet still had the feeling of hunger inside.

While floating, Vinnie remembered his mother opening her beak to him and projecting delicious chunks of rich fish oils and eggs. It flowed from her beak to his when he was too young to fly and find his own food. He remembered how excited he had been when he saw her fly toward him. He knew that she would bring him food and peck his down fuzz. He would peck her beak to beg for more. She would bend forward, again bringing some delicious morsels. That was such a lazy life, waiting for his mother or father to come open their beaks to deliver squid or gruel of some fish-egg mixture that they had carried from far out to sea and back to him.

https://youtu.be/_6aQHlUu0Ws

His mother would stand by him, admiring how he would try to walk to her, with legs not quite strong enough to hold him. She would step away from him a little, and he would have to try harder to move toward her. She would peck him at the itchy places that he could not reach. Most of all he remembered how his mother and father would just stand and admire him. He could not understand why she would not come to his aid when he would get into a fight with other chicks. Sometimes another mother, while working up enough venom to bring up the last bit of food for her chick, would come to beat up on him. His mother would not intervene during these painful attacks, either.

He remembered one time when his mother had brought him food that was hard and long and difficult to swallow. The hard thing stayed in his stomach for a long time and caused him pain when he bent over or moved his neck in a certain way. Now that he was older he could cough it up and get rid of the irritation, but until then he had to endure the pain it caused because he was not strong enough to expel it. He remembered that some of the chicks around him became weaker and weaker if they could not expel their hard thing. When a chick was fed something that was not edible, it would feel pain and not beg for food. In reaction to not begging, the parent would not bring up food for it. Soon the chick folded its wings, put its head down, and did not move again.

Its mom and dad no longer came to it.

https://youtu.be/TyzXazKe8y4

For more visuals of remains of dead birds, Google "MIDWAY ISLAND, North Pacific Ocean," and click on "Unbelievable U Tube," at 3:04 minutes, by photographic artist Chris Jordan.

He liked it best when both his mother and father were together. They would sit in front of the nest and gently peck at each other to scratch or to smooth feathers. They would put their beaks into their backs, which held their oil glands, and rub some new oils into their head or neck feathers to help keep them afloat on the water.

Vinnie was always fascinated by how the rain rolled off his parent's backs. As a chick, when he got wet, his fuzzy coat just got soaked. The more it rained, the wetter he became. When the wind was cold as well as the rain, he would shiver. If it rained very hard, he might stay in a puddle for days shivering. Those chicks that had nests on the low level where water pools would sit for days in the water, fearing to leave their nests. In some cases, they would drown in the puddles within the nests.

https://youtu.be/kmbx1fcWdgw

Vinnie was alone. He had been alone on the sea for almost four years now. He looked off into the distance, and still he did not see another bird. He thought how nice it would be nice to sit beside another bird like himself and have her scratch his neck and put some oil on his feathers. He would like to reach into his oil gland and put some oil on some other bird, just as he remembered his parents doing. He remembered how his parents would sit facing each other and rest their necks together. He would like to have a bird like himself peck his chest and coo softly. He would like to dance and peck and holler. He would like to have a son like himself to admire and share some of his food with. He would like to have another bird to admire his magnificent chest of feathers and his grand wingspan that could lift him easily into the sky and swoop again in an effortless manner.

This longing for home and a family of his own must be the restless feeling that had been haunting him and could not be silenced with food or flight. It was time for Vinnie to mate and have a son of his own. He was a long way from home and would have to fly thousands of miles to reach there. Vinnie remembered that the winds could take him to the place where he was born.

He knew that he could fight any bird for a plot of land. He knew that he could woo and win a handsome hen that would admire him for his strength and beauty. He knew that he must return to the place of his birth from whence he came, and that he must start off soon. He would take his fill from the sea, rest until light came again, and then begin his journey. Vinnie was going home.

CHAPTER 3
The Homecoming

• • •

SEVERAL DAYS PASSED AS VINNIE winged his way home, directed by instincts. He took -very little time to eat or rest. His flight was almost effortless, like hitch hiking on the wind at sea. Finally, in the distance he could see a thin familiar outline of an island emerging from the smooth ocean surface.

His heart raced and he flapped his wings faster to speed his journey. He began to make out the color change in the water where the surf beats against the land.

Other birds came into view from all directions, each heading toward the island. Colors began to emerge from the land. There was the brown from the dreaded ironwood trees, where Vinnie had seen many birds caught hanging from branches and dying helplessly. There was green from the naupaka bushes and the white sand of the beaches coming into view.

Vinnie circled the island to enjoy the familiar view of the lagoon. All around him flying birds speckled the sky. Birds of all kind covered the ground. There were the shearwaters and the petrels, the frigate birds and the masked boobies, the tropic birds, the terns, and the noddies, all returning to build their nests.

https://youtu.be/HPvItUiVAlE

Vinnie flew over these groups of birds and then saw his familiar territory. He let his feet drag and lowered his tail to slow his speed. He hit the ground hard, and his head and beak smashed into the dirt first, causing severe pain. He flipped over his feet several times and then came to a stop. He lay there a few minutes then struggled to his feet. His parents saw Vinnie land and were happy to see him.

He had flown to the exact spot where he had been born. He surveyed the twenty feet around the nest where he had waited obediently for many months for his parents to return from their long flights and bring food back from the sea to him. His parents were rebuilding their nest. His father was pretending to help at first and then lost interest and walked away to watch his mother finish. His mother must have known just how she wanted the nest to look, and his father was just in the way. He had more important things to do anyway, like walk around to inspect the surroundings. She inspected Vinnie's beak gently. She rubbed his neck and then went back to building her nest. She felt sorry that he was hurt, but she had pressing things to do right now, building her nest. Vinnie was her chick, but no longer her responsibility. He must make it on his own. She wished him well and then forgot about him as she returned to her task at hand. Vinnie was happy to be home.

Happily, he waddled across the field. A young male bird squealed and pecked at him, fearful that Vinnie would threaten his territory. Vinnie moved on, respectful, but unafraid. He did not care. It was a beautiful day and he was home at last.

Across the field Vinnie saw a group of young birds involved in a mating dance. Vinnie walked over to join them. They were rubbing each other's bills and then clacking. They would lift their wings and peck under first one wing and then the other. They would then walk around in a circle on their toes.

Every once in a while, they would put their heads back into the air, let out a wild howl, and then repeat their maneuver over again. There may be two or three or sometimes four dancing in a circle, each displaying their talent.

Vinnie walked over to a group, which readily accepted him into their circle. One young chick approached and clicked bills with him. There was a searing pain in his beak, so he backed away. The hen was startled but didn't mind; there were other birds to dance with. He took great joy in stepping forward with one foot and then the other. He did this for several moments, taking full pride with each step. He practiced raising his weight upon his toes. This was so neat to rise up on his toes. He threw his head back and let out a howl of joy. Vinnie watched the other birds from a distance, enjoying their wild posturing. It looked like so much fun. He was really glad he had come home.

This is where he belonged, among his own. It felt strange walking on something solid. He had been on the water for most of his life. Something solid beneath his feet was a new experience for him.

When he resumed his prancing, he saw before him a beautiful chick. She was looking at him with amazement that he was howling all by himself. She would show him how he was supposed to dance and *then* howl. Advancing toward Vinnie, she carefully brushed her beak against his. He pulled back remembering the pain. She did not understand why such a handsome bird would not want to dance with her. She approached him again and gently brushed her beak against his. Her gentle touch felt very good to Vinnie so he gently brushed his beak against hers. The discomfort was worth the feeling he would describe as a "quickening." She began a rhythmical bill pecking against his and then a clacking of her own. She would lift one wing, ceremoniously peck under her wing, then walk around in a circle on her toes, and then let out a howl. That thrilled Vinnie. He repeated her dance, taking pleasure in the wing pecking and prancing on his toes around the circle, and especially the howl, but he did not want to repeat the bill pecking or even the bill clapping, for this was painful.

When he did not respond to her bill clicking, she stepped back and stood still. She then looked away, and walked off. Vinnie wanted to follow her, but stood and put his head down. Soon there was another chick before him. Gently she pressed her bill against his. Vinnie pecked under his wing and then walked on his toes and let out a howl startling the young chick. Who ever heard of finishing a dance before starting it? She thought that this must be a strange fellow and walked away.

Several groups of birds were gathered, practicing the dance with grace and joy. When one pair of birds would dance particularly well together, they would begin to exclude other birds who would try to enter their dance. It was as if the other birds did not exist. Sometimes two or three other birds would aggressively try to enter this couple's dance, but the partners would continue as if there were no others present. Soon the graceful couple would leave the dance area and go to the male bird's "territory," and begin to construct a simple nest. Meanwhile the other birds would continue to dance with one or several partners until they found one that had pleasing and graceful movements that meshed with their own.

Vinnie walked around watching the dancing and nest building. He saw the black-footed birds with the black chests also danced. They did the same introductory bill clicking, bill clapping, and the wing tucks, but theirs was a different dance. The difference was that the black-footed birds would make larger sweeps with their bills, clack louder, and prance higher, and when they pecked under their wings, they would spread both their wings and their tails and let out a loud honking noise. Vinnie thought these black-footed birds were too aggressive. When one of the black-footed birds approached him, he would look away and continue on. He preferred the gentle graceful dance of his own kind.

He watched how pairs would build a nest. The white-chested Laysan would move inland and look for soft and higher ground. She would find bits of twigs and grasses and then form a circle with them.

The hen would then sit in the middle of the circle and move around to push the twigs out toward the edges and make the body cavity deep. She would refine the nest by gathering bits of dirt, feathers, leaves, and pine needles, and again nestle in the middle until satisfied she had a nice soft place for an egg and room to sit upon it. The black-footed birds usually built their nest closer to the sea, on sand, or at the edge of the dunes. Their nests were usually shallower and held fewer materials.

One bird that Vinnie watched had a chest that was both white and black. Its head was somewhat white and the feet were black. This bird would approach a white-chested Laysan and peck bills and try to dance, but the dance was too aggressive for the Laysan. He would then wander over to a black-footed pair and try to join the dance. He would prance and howl like the others, but he didn't quite have the right motions or the proper honk. They, too, would walk away from him. This multicolored bird would then stand alone and watch the others continue to dance. Soon he was not attempting to join anymore. Vinnie felt his sadness and his need to join the dance. He walked over and stood beside him, but felt no need to dance. Soon the other bird walked away from him and he was again alone.

Perhaps tomorrow he would again try to click bills and join the others, but for today, he would just watch and learn. Tomorrow was another day and he was glad to be home.

https://youtu.be/KFvUw-TcNlY

CHAPTER 4
Why Is It Important?

• • •

IN THE MORNING VINNIE WATCHED his mother gather twigs. He approached her with the question he had been thinking about all night.

"Why is it important to dance?"

Vinnie's mother saw the pain in his beautiful face. She leaned over to him and brushed his neck with her bill.

She said, "Vinnie, the dance is our way to find out who can work well together. When the movements are harmonious and pleasant, there is a greater chance that the nest will be successful. The dance tests the partner for strength, and vigor, and grace to ensure that their offspring would also be strong and vigorous. A female albatross is looking for a mate to mingle with her seed. She wants a mate that is strong and capable of sharing the duties of caring for their offspring. She wants one that can synchronize with her movements, one that would be compatible and that she could look forward to being around for a long time. Essentially, she wants the bravest, brightest, healthiest, and most graceful, talented bird she can find to be her mate. He must be equal to her in beauty and ability to perform. Dance is the way we test each other to select a companion. The answer must be yes to so many questions you ask, such as: Are their movements pleasing to one another? Does it feel good to dance with this other bird? Do they like to repeat the dance together? Do they want to join in when the partner is dancing with another? Does one bird excite them more than another, and do they feel the quickening?"

She stared out into space and said, "Vinnie, when you feel the quickening, you will know that you have found your mate. For us, the dance is how we find these things. This is why it is important."

Vinnie listened intently. He knew she was telling the truth. He hung his head and shuffled his feet.

His mother looked at his beak and understood his problem. She wanted to help him, but did not know how.

His mother looked at him sympathetically. "Come over to the edge of the field, child, and I will show you how other birds find their mates. Do you see those beautiful white birds with the long red tails? They are tropic birds that come to nest on this island as well. When they find another bird they feel is worthy to carry their seed, they fly a mating flight that is a beautiful sight to behold. They will dive, and climb, and swoop, change directions, and then almost stall as one. They are demonstrating to each other their fitness and their ability to work together, their joy at being together and having found a worthy partner. Observe, son, the beauty of their dance."

Vinnie carefully watched the flight of the red-tailed birds. He envied their graceful dance. He knew he could fly it easily for days with his large, powerful wings. He could swoop, dive, climb, and qualify as a great mate as a red-tailed bird, but he could not stand the pain that bill clacking required of his own kind.

Vinnie thought for a moment and then said to his mother, "Why can't I show a mate how powerful and trustworthy I can be, how worthy a mate

I am, by taking a bird on a flight like this? Why wouldn't they feel the quickening in this way? We would work together, showing our agility, vigor, and strength. I would build a great nest and take good care of my chick. I am graceful, young, and healthy. Why can't they see that I would make a good mate, see the strength and beauty that is in me without the dance? I would nurture our chick, bring back food for him, sit with the nest, and protect my family. I am brave and ready to give my love and be filled with love. Why can't they see this? Why can't they see who I am without the dance?"

His mother looked at him sympathetically and said, "Vinnie, the dance is our way. You will have to follow it, or you will not have a partner to share your life and what that sharing brings." She looked at him and understood why he would find the dance painful. She felt sorry for him, but to do other than the dance was indeed a strange idea. She said, "Vinnie, this is the way it is."

She returned to her nest making with a worried frown, and made a note to talk to his father about Vinnie's problem.

After watching the red-tailed birds for a long time, Vinnie found his father and posed the same question he had asked his mother.

"Father," said Vinnie, "Why is it important to dance?" He expected his father to give him a sensible explanation, one he could accept.

His father looked at him, not expecting such a question from his own son. He said without hesitation, "Vinnie, this is the way we males show our mates that we want them to join us and that we really do care for them. When we find the right mate, we need to have a way to show her that we are strong, agile, caring, soft, yet firm. Through the dance we show her that she can trust us to help her raise the family. It would be safe for her to trust you to help raise your family. When you feel the quickening you will want to lead your mate to the nesting place that you have chosen to nurture your young. She needs to know that you are dependable, and capable of taking care of them. That is the way it is."

Vinnie understood what his father way saying. He didn't like the answer, but he understood.

"Father," said Vinnie, "What is this 'quickening' that you and mother describe?"

His father said, "Vinnie, when you dance, some birds follow your movements. They begin to mimic your own movements, and the dance is graceful. You will enjoy the dance and recognize those with whom you can work easily. You are together in your thoughts and are pleasing to each other. The dance becomes more exciting and pleasurable, and there is an ease of movement. The quickening comes like a jolt that begins in your throat and goes through your body. When you feel the quickening, you know you have found the mate that you will keep for life."

Vinnie looked out and saw partners moving. Some were halting in the dance, and some were smooth. Those that were smooth continued to dance. In other cases the partners lost interest and walked away to find other partners.

Vinnie looked wistfully at the birds with the red tails and then back at his own kind. He closed his eyes while his mind swirled with the realization that he must dance. There was no other way, pain or no pain.

"Perhaps I should look for a nesting site first," thought Vinnie. He figured that at least this first step would not be painful. He began to scout the area near his parents' home site. He considered several sites, but at last he spotted a site that seemed just right. It was near the beach for the run to the sea. It was far enough away from the sand, so that when the wind blew, it would not blow sand onto the chick and into the nest. It was near a naupaka bush for shade from the blistering sun. It was on high ground, so that when the rains came, the chick would not have to sit in a puddle of water.

Vinnie was quite happy with his selection. It was close to a food source and seemed a place to raise a family. He surveyed his site with pleasure, when suddenly two male birds flew down and walked up to him. They began to push him and peck at him. Apparently they also found this spot pleasing and wanted it for their own. This was his site and he felt ready to fight for it.

When both birds charged him, Vinnie stood his ground. The intruders made loud noises while pecking him with their beaks and beating him with their wings. Vinnie spread his wings and flew above them, striking them again and again with his feet and chest. He made loud noises and butted his head against them. They pecked and he butted. His best tactic was to fly above them and come down with his feet, and charge with his head down, ramming them with his chest over and over. He was determined not to leave this choice piece of ground. Vinnie seemed to gain strength as he fought.

The other birds were puzzled by this strange bird who did not fight as they were used to fighting. The two finally walked away, thinking another spot might be easier to obtain. Vinnie was big and strong, and not afraid to defend his ground. He strutted on his hill, strengthened from the fight and having proven his courage.

https://youtu.be/dSJpFrU3JWQ

CHAPTER 5

Hester

• • •

ON A NEARBY HILL ABOVE him, a young female had been watching Vinnie defend his territory. She was struck by the bravery of this handsome male. She felt a quickening, and spread her wings and made a fluttering sound. Looking up, Vinnie saw a beautiful female admiring him. Walking up the hill, he bowed his head in greeting. Pleased to have him notice her, Hester again felt the thrill of quickening.

Hester was just four years old, like Vinnie. She had watched the dance and knew what to do. She began to lift up on her toes and prance around Vinnie. He did likewise. This was most enjoyable to him. They eyed each other, and she hesitatingly reached out her bill to touch his. The touch was soft and pleasurable.

He responded by touching her bill and then pecking under his wing, as the dance required. This was pleasurable. Vinnie let out a howl, and this too was pleasurable. He pecked softly again, clacked his bill, and then rose up on his toes and danced around. He then pecked his other wing underside and let out another howl. She repeated his movements, and then they howled together.

Vinnie was dancing. This female was gentle and rhythmical. She was mimicking his movements with grace. They were in unison. They began a sinuous walk. It felt so good to be dancing. As the dance became more intense, he began to feel the pain, but he could not stop. He felt the quickening.

Pain was mixed with pleasure and the quickening felt more certain. Vinnie was dancing. He had found his mate! But after two more patterns, the hot pain that seared through him was almost blinding.

Vinnie stopped; he could not go on.

Hester stood bewildered. How could this perfect dance have ended so abruptly?

She approached Vinnie again and softly touched his bill. Vinnie jumped back, turning away from her. Dizzy with pain, he staggered backward. He saw the blur of the sea in the distance. He stumbled to the top of the sand hill and with a few running steps launched himself into the air.

He needed to be alone.

As he flew away, a stricken Hester watched him go. She stared after Vinnie, not believing what she was seeing. Their movements had been so perfect together, she had felt the quickening. She had thought this brave fighter and gentle dancer would stay with her forever.

She walked in the sand, following Vinnie's path in the sky, expecting to see him return at any moment. She saw nothing else around her. With Vinnie gone, she continued to walk down the beach in the direction she had seen him last, always looking up into the sky.

Suddenly, Hester found herself surrounded by a group of young black-footed birds. They surrounded her and begged to dance, frightening her with their rapid and exaggerated movements. Hester tried to walk away, but they were young and full of the spirit of the dance. They wanted to dance, and each pecked at her and spread their wings and pranced on their toes. As the birds surrounded her, she felt breathless and just folded her legs beneath her. They pecked at her and howled. When she did not respond to them, they became more aggressive. One after the other, they sexually attacked her. They were very rough, first defiling her, and then leaving Hester on the beach broken and bloodied.

https://youtu.be/ahuS3m-7x_A

Filled with rage and humiliation, Hester lay panting on the beach. Through her tears, she could see the birds off in the distance still selecting partners and hear their wild howls.

She lay there until the sun rose over the hill and then struggled up the sand to her home. She was physically spent and emotionally exhausted, but more important, she was "with egg."

She did not know why she was no longer interested in the dance. She merely stood and backed away from the others. She felt salt running down her nostrils when she had not taken seawater. Her heart was heavy, her body wracked, and she no longer felt the joy of the howl.

Hester folded her wings and legs under her white chest and just stared into space. She did not feel like eating or drinking or moving about. She did not notice the others dancing and did not respond when others came up to invite her to dance. When the wind blew, Hester did not turn her body into the wind, and her feathers were ruffled. She did not move when the rain came, and she was surrounded by a puddling of water.

After several days, she walked to the seashore. Later, Hester ran down the hill to work up enough speed to fly. She did eat some, but returned to the hill shortly. She looked over to where Vinnie had defended his parcel of the earth. Vinnie was nowhere in sight now. Hester began to gather some twigs and grass and started forming a nest. She began to feel heavy in the groin and knew that she was "with egg."

With a heavy heart, she began to prepare her nest, and she sat upon it without joy. She knew that, without a mate, she would abandon the nest. One parent alone could never raise a chick to full maturation. She knew that this unborn chick was doomed and that she had only one egg to bear. She felt defeated and sad, and she was becoming very angry. Her dream of having a strong and beautiful mate with whom she could build a future was gone. She knew that it was their way to mate for life and that no one would want to mate with her if she were "with egg."

Feeling hungry, Hester walked to the hill and ran down it to gather speed. It was more of a waddle than a run, for the egg was heavy now. She stayed out to sea for a few days, and when she returned, she stood still, shocked by what she saw. Scattered all over the ground was what remained of the meager nest that she had made. Not a feather or grass blade remained. There was scratching into the dirt where the nest had been. Who would do such a terrible thing? How could she continue to live?

"Do not I deserve more than this?" she thought.

Hester looked at the sky as if there would be an answer from there. With a heavy heart she began to rebuild the nest, preparing to defend it no matter what happened. She rarely slept now, for one eye was always open for intruders.

Hester thought about the toll that bringing forth an egg would take on her body. She would willingly bear that with a mate, who would share in the joy of bringing a chick into the world that they could nurture together and watch with pride the growth and the beauty that they had both brought forth.

It was a sad Hester who laid her egg a few weeks later and sat upon it for a few days. She stood up, pecked at her egg, and tried to roll it over. In the nest next to her, a hen who had just laid her egg was being nudged aside by the father to leave and go regenerate at sea. Another across the way was returning from the sea after resting and feeding. She was nudging her mate off the nest so he, too, could go to sea to feed. As Hester looked around, she saw many other birds trading places. One mate after the other would sit on the nest, keeping the egg warm while the other went out to sea to regenerate. Her egg would die when it was not kept warm.

Hester pecked at her egg and rolled it with her beak. As if the egg could hear she spoke to it, saying, "If I stay here with you to keep you warm, we shall both die. I cannot keep you alive by myself, so now I must go. I am so sorry. Please forgive me." Hester waited and listened, as if expecting the reply she knew would never come.

With a heavy heart, Hester walked to the top of the sand hill. She took one look back and then ran down the hill to gain the lift for flight, planning to never return again to this place of sadness.

CHAPTER 6
Vinnie Returns

• • •

AFTER SEVERAL WEEKS AT SEA, Vinnie returned to the island. He circled the familiar lagoon, pleased to see the fields, with many thousands of nests now bulging with an egg and attentive parents. He flew over to check out his own place on the island.

Shocked, he found a nest built on his site. He fluttered above his spot in disbelief. Anger flooded throughout him. Diving down to the nest, he scratched all the feathers and grass away from the plot. He angrily obliterated any trace of nest that remained, threw his head back, and howled. He was prepared to fight any challengers. When none came forward, Vinnie decided to retreat to the top of the hill and wait for the intruder. He would then confront him, making him rue the day he stole this spot.

Vinnie picked a good vantage point on the hill above the nest and waited. It was a full day before he saw a bird stumble to a halt in front of his spot and walk up to the area he had marked as his. Could this really be who he thought it was? Was that Hester in his nest?

He did not attack the intruder as he had planned to do. He watched in amazement as Hester went about putting the nest back together. Vinnie waited to see who would join her. What kind of bird had won the partner he would have chosen? Several days went by, and no one came. He waited.

When Hester bore her egg, she did not leave her nest like the other birds. No male bird came to relieve her. One day Vinnie watched Hester get up, roll her egg, and then leave her nest and fly away.

He knew that the egg must be kept warm and could not believe that Hester would just leave her egg.

From the hill, Vinnie watched the egg all that day, and no male sat upon it. When nightfall came, Vinnie was very uncomfortable and could not bear to see Hester's egg so badly treated. Vinnie walked down to the nest and nudged the egg. It was still warm. He looked around to see if anyone was coming. There was no one.

He walked up to the nest, stood over the egg, gently lowered his legs to place his featherless incubation patch over it, and closed his eyes.

This was not his egg, but somehow it felt right. It was Hester's egg, and it would die if he did not tend to it. Vinnie knew that the mating dance was the way to select a mate and that the pain was too great for him to complete the dance. Protecting Hester's egg was the way he could prove to her all the important things that were being tested in the mating dance. He could show her that he was faithful, capable of protecting and caring for her and their young. He repeated to himself his father's advice: "You have got to show her that you want her."

Vinnie was feeling very possessive, but he was getting very hungry. He did not leave to fly, or to eat. Sitting on that egg seemed such a natural thing to do. He enjoyed the feel of the egg on his patch of skin. It felt warm, and he was sure he could feel it move occasionally. When he felt it move, he would speak to it gently with an "eh, eh, eh" sound. He wasn't sure why he did this, but it felt right.

"You need to talk to your young and let them know who their parents are," he reasoned.

He looked around and saw many nests now with the male bird keeping the egg warm. The females needed to regenerate after separating from the egg. They would go out to sea to feed for a couple of weeks and then return to relieve their mates to do the same.

As the sun rose, Vinnie watched hundreds of birds marching by him on their way to the hill to fly out to feed and bring back food for their chicks.

https://youtu.be/biqO9VUlzXg

Vinnie saw some of the females return to relieve their mates next to him and waited patiently for Hester to return. He was hungry, but he knew that Hester would be glad to see that he had kept the egg warm with his body. She would be along shortly to relieve him. He closed his eyes and waited.

The nest next to him was now occupied again by the male, who had gone out to feed and returned.

He was feeling very hungry and could feel his ribs against the egg now in place of his chest. He was losing his bulk, but still he sat on the egg. He saw the males and females exchange all around him, but Hester did not return to relieve him.

Vinnie began to wonder if something had happened to Hester. The thought struck him that maybe Hester never meant to return. Was he here to die sitting on this egg that did not belong to him? If he left this egg, which he had nurtured for weeks now, it would die if there were no one to tend to it.

Then again, he would die if he did not go out to feed. Hunger gnawed at him.

"What am I supposed to do?"

Vinnie stood up and walked around the nest. His legs were wobbly, and his joints were stiff. This did not feel good. He looked at Hester's egg and then looked out to sea, where he knew he would find nourishment. He wondered if he could leave for just a little while. The egg looked so help-less, and he knew Hester would be disappointed in him if he did not keep his vigil. He needed to show her that he wanted her, and this was his way.

Vinnie again straddled the nest and again placed his featherless spot over the egg. He closed his eyes and dreamed of flying off to sea. He dreamed of swallowing large clumps of fish eggs and seawater at the same time. He would again be the big proud bird he had been.

With his great wingspan and large chest, he could do anything and go anywhere. But now Vinnie dropped his head; he could no longer hold it up. He slept because he was too tired and weak to dream anymore. His breathing became shallow and rapid, and his body was limp.

The sun came up. Vinnie was very hungry. He dreamed of seeing Hester standing above him, stroking his head and nudging him off of the nest and taking his place. He dreamed that Hester had returned and that he was free to go to sea. He thought he felt the egg move. He raised his head, and the world turned. He tried to stand, and his feet would not hold him. He dreamed that Hester had gently opened his beak and poured a delicious oil into his bill. He swallowed and dreamed that he had never tasted anything so delicious. She opened his beak again, and again she poured in some fish parts, and he swallowed. Vinnie then fell into a deep sleep.

CHAPTER 7
Hester's Choice

• • •

A HEALTHIER HESTER RETURNED TO the island. When she had left her nest, she had planned to never return. She had spent many weeks at sea, bathing, eating, resting, healing. One day she was overcome with longing, a tender, sad longing that guided her path back to Vinnie's site.

From the air, it appeared that her nest was occupied by what appeared to be a dead bird. She came closer, landing directly in front of the nest.

"Vinnie, is that you?" she asked. There was no answer. Hester nudged the slack body and saw that the egg under him was very much alive. Her primary concern was for Vinnie. She bent over him and stroked his feathers. His shallow breathing moved his sides against the dirt and grass. He let out a moan, and she felt his warm neck with her beak. She pried his beak apart, put her beak into his, and then brought forth some oils and fish she had stored in her gullet.

Vinnie stirred and slowly swallowed. He opened his eyes and lifted his head for a moment. Again Hester pecked his beak, and Vinnie opened it. She poured fresh oils and fish eggs into his beak again.

Vinnie swallowed.

Hester nudged Vinnie off the nest. As Vinnie rolled to one side, she moved into position over the egg. With him beside her, she could stroke and feed Vinnie while she sat on the egg.

Hours passed, and when the sun rose again, Vinnie blinked and opened his eyes. Hester was sitting on the egg. He leaned over to touch her. He could feel the vibrant beak and chest of Hester and smell the salt air of the sea and the oils that had spilled from his beak. This was no dream. Hester had returned. Vinnie wobbled to his feet. He maneuvered to the top of the hill and ran down to gather speed. Soon he was airborne. Once he was in the air, he felt alive and happy. He had done his job, and he was still alive. He would eat his fill, and he felt his wings beat joyously again.

When he returned to the island after a week, he did not know what to expect. Hester was sitting on the egg. She showered him with pecks and nudges and gave up her place for Vinnie to sit. This was their egg; the two of them would bring this chick into the world. When it was time for Hester to go to sea again, she returned quickly, and they remained together for a while, taking turns nurturing their treasure.

"What a courageous bird you are, Vinnie," she said. "You were about to give your life for this chick."

"I thought you were never going to return. Why did you stay away so long?" Vinnie asked.

"I was planning to never return, and I nearly did not," admitted Hester. "You see, I did not have a mate to help me bring forth this chick."

"Then how did you become with egg? How did this happen?" asked Vinnie.

Hester put her head down and told him the story of how she had followed him down the beach when he flew away and how she had wandered into a group of young black-footed birds.

Vinnie reached out to her and stroked hear head with his beak. He put his neck around hers, and they sat quietly for a long time.

"We will bring this chick into the world, and it will be one of the bravest birds in all creation. It will need all the strength that we can give it." Vinnie gazed into Hester's eyes with the black patches beneath. "Hester, we will have many more years to bring forth great birds, and each year should be better than the year before."

"You are the mate every hen yearns for," said Hester. "This proven dedication to our nest is what every hen is trying to discover in the dance. How fortunate I am to have discovered you."

Vinnie rose and breathed deeply, his chest expanding with joy and pride.

"I have complete faith and trust in you, Vinnie. You have proven your worth." She nuzzled him softly.

https://youtu.be/kmbx1fcWdgw

Over the next weeks, Vinnie went out to feed for only short periods. He liked the attention that Hester paid to him. He was happiest when he was sitting on or near the nest with Hester by his side.

He had found his mate, and for now he would be happy to bring food back to his chick as if it were his own.

One day when he came back to the nest after feeding, he was surprised to see Hester off the nest.

She was bending over the egg, just looking at it. He walked over and stood beside her.

"Look, Vinnie, the egg is starting to crack," murmured Hester. "I can feel the chick trying to get out. It is trying so hard; can't we help by cracking the egg to make the journey easier?"

https://youtu.be/Y7SvJKB5wOM

Stepping in front of her, he cautioned, "No, Hester, our chick must make it out on its own. If it isn't strong enough to survive the birth, it should not live. That is the way it is."

Hester looked at him and then back at the egg. She stood resolute. The two of them waited to see the progress while the pecking inside the egg continued and then stopped. Hester glanced at Vinnie but did not move. Moving closer, Vinnie put his ear to the egg and then stepped back.

"I am sure it is just resting," Vinnie said.

A few moments later, the pecking began again, and a small crack appeared. It was quiet for a short time, and then the pecking began again. The crack widened. The two of them stood quietly watching and listening for every movement. A large crack appeared on the egg, and a black knob on a small pink bill appeared and then disappeared. More pecking and wider cracks now were appearing. At last a fuzzy head appeared, soon followed by a shoulder. The chick lay spent for what seemed a long time.

"Surely we can help it now that it has shown it can escape from the egg," Hester pleaded.

Vinnie cautioned her not to interfere. "If it cannot get itself out of the egg, it should not live," Vinnie said sternly.

Cruel as it seemed, Hester knew that he was right. She waited. Shortly, her excitement grew as the head began to stir, and then the neck emerged from the egg and then the *black feet*.

The feet. Hester looked at Vinnie, who saw the feet at the same time. They looked at each other and then back to the chick. Vinnie did not say a word. He turned and walked toward the hill to the sea.

Soon he was airborne.

Hester looked after him with concern. She went about brushing up her chick. She made her nest more comfortable and sat down beside him.

"I shall call you Victor," said Hester. "Welcome to the world; I am glad you are here." Hester knew that Victor could not understand what she was saying, but she wanted to let him know that he was loved and would be cared for.

She was relieved to see Vinnie appear a short time later. He walked over to the chick, spread his beak, and poured oil and fish eggs into its beak. The excited chick begged for more. Vinnie obliged.

Watching, Hester knew then that this nest would be successful. She flew off happily to get more food for a hungry chick that was already bigger than most in their surrounding area.

CHAPTER 8

Victor

• • •

https://youtu.be/ylcyUeNVQt0

VICTOR BURST INTO THE WORLD hungry. He would peck vigorously at Vinnie and Hester each time they arrived with food. He would devour each beak full and come back greedily for more. It took the hard work of both parents to satisfy their growing chick. Vinnie liked it best when there was time for him and Hester to sit beside the nest and groom each other. They would sit with their necks entwined.

Hester would step back and admire both Vinnie and her chick. At other times Vinnie would stand over both of them and survey the hillside as if he did not notice they both were looking at him.

Victor was standing in his nest long before the other chicks could hold themselves up. At first Victor's size stirred a little jealousy among the other parents. The murmurs and laughter began when Victor began to wobble walk outside the nest.

"Look at the black feet on that chick. No wonder he is so much bigger and so lusty. He is not one of us," said one neighbor.

"Too bad about that dud in your nest," said another. "I didn't know you had it in you."

"Are you the one who almost died bringing this monster into the world?" asked another.

"No wonder your hen didn't come back," said another. "She probably knew what was in there."

Vinnie would ignore the taunts, but he was beginning to get angry; this was a chick to be proud of, and he would not hear otherwise. He said to Hester, "This lovely chick that you bore is going to get the best food and training that is possible to provide a chick. He will fledge and go out to sea to live a fruitful life, but you know that he will never dance. The dance is not everything. Victor is so healthy and vigorous; he will find so much in the world to enjoy."

When Hester went out to feed and gather with the other parents on the lagoon to sun and socialize, the neighbor hens would snicker and swim away from her. They would gather again at another place.

Victor, too, began to question his parents. "What is it about me that is so different? Why do the other chicks laugh and walk away from me and yell 'freak of nature, freak of nature'?"

Hester knew that she must answer these questions. She walked over to him and smoothed the top of his fuzzy head and stroked his beak gently. She stood over him and said, "Life is not always as you would like it to be." She went on, "Wherever you go, you must be able to find the good and the best of whatever or wherever you are and be successful in ignoring the worst and the bad. Learn to actively search for and appreciate the positives in whatever you do, for that is way to find happiness."

"But why do they laugh at me?"

"When the other chicks laugh at you, Victor, you can choose to think of some of your private pleasures," said Hester. "You can develop an ability to enjoy the simple things and the obvious that others might not even see because they are too busy to notice."

Victor said he would practice what she had taught him, but somehow things did not feel fair to him.

Vinnie watched his son grow daily. He had magnificent wingspan and sturdy legs. His chest was full, and his eyes were bright. He learned quickly. Vinnie would sit beside his son and talk to him.

Victor would ask, "Why am I different?"

"Well, son, there are a variety of ways that a bird comes into this world. Your birth was different from most, but that did not make you any less worthy. Because you are different, you will be able to fly faster and farther than any of your cousins. You will be able to catch fish and eggs more easily. You will be able to defend yourself better than any around. You will be able to fly higher and see more. The strongest wind will be your friend."

Victor drank all this good news in and then asked, "Will I have any bird friends?"

Vinnie thought for a long time and then answered, "Perhaps."

Victor did not like the long delay in his father's answer. "It is not fair if I don't have any friends just because my feet are black. What does having black feet have to do with anything?"

His father drew a deep breath. "Victor, the black feet are not so much of a problem as what is about to happen to you,"

Victor's eyes widened. "What else could happen to me?"

"Your chick fuzz is black like the other chicks now, but as we speak, that fuzz is being pushed out by maturing feathers," his father went on. "Your black fuzz is being replaced by black-and-white feathers, while the other chicks' fuzz is being replaced by all-white feathers. Both are good, but different."

"Oh, father," cried Victor, "that is really unfair. Why did this happen to me?"

His father thought for a long time before answering. "Victor, life is not fair, and no one should expect that it should be."

The answer surprised Victor, and he waited for his father to explain more.

"Look at my beak. It was not fair that a hook should be placed on a squid that was floating on top of the water so that my beak got hooked on it, causing me great pain and almost killing me."

Victor took a closer look at Vinnie's beak and pecked at it. His father had always fed him from the right side while his mother fed him from both sides. Now he knew why.

Vinnie went on. "It was not fair to that squid that he be hooked and fastened to a line. It was not fair that I should be fooled into thinking that a floating squid in the middle of the sea was good food when it was really a trap."

Victor nodded.

"You see, son," Vinnie went on, "the 'not fair' tag is like a clump of seaweed wrapped around your foot when you are trying to fly or even walk. Don't drag it around with you. You will not only have trouble getting off the ground, but you are also liable to catch it on something below you when you are trying to fly. It will hang you up or drag you down. Don't attach yourself to some long seaweed."

Victor looked at his feet and could imagine seaweed hanging off. He certainly did not want to be dragging anything like that around.

Vinnie said, "What would *really* be unfair would be for you to leave this island focusing on what could have been rather than what is possible."

He saw that Victor was listening. "When the time comes for you to go into the world, you will need all the strength and skill that you can muster to survive. It is up to you to learn all you can. You have great strengths. Recognize all of them, build on them, and never look back at what you think might not be fair."

Victor looked at his father for a long time and then looked out to sea. He began to think about all the things that he could do that the other chicks could not. He looked at his black feet and thought about being able to walk around while other chicks were still helpless in their nests.

The following day, Victor noticed that he could shoot his effluvia [chewed-up food] farther than any around. He took great relish at being able to aim and shoot at just the right time in the right direction.

Victor noticed something else that made him proud. When parents came to feed their chicks and had trouble bringing up the last bit, they would go to a neighboring nest and beat up on the chick inside. The excitement stimulated them enough to go back to their own nest to feed their chick their last morsel. When such parents saw Victor standing tall in his nest, they usually looked for an easier target, leaving him alone. Victor watched other chicks being beaten up by a feeding mother and remembered his father's words about life not being fair.

When there was laughter as he grew, he became adept at thinking of advantages that made him a survivor. He walked tall, his black-and-white feathers shining in the sun.

CHAPTER 9
The School of Hard Knocks

• • •

EARLY ONE MORNING VINNIE MARCHED to the sand hill for the regular run to flight. That day he was among the first to fly from the island to go to sea. As he passed over parts of the island, he looked down to see many thousands of birds marching to the sand hill. They, too, would bring back life-giving nutrients for their young in their internal pouches. Vinnie felt himself part of the ongoing stream of life, one larger than his single self.

When Vinnie returned with his precious cargo, he landed skillfully near the nest. Victor was gone.

"Victor," he called. There was no answer. "Hester," he called. Still there was no answer.

Vinnie began to panic. He fluttered around the surrounding nests, searching for Victor.

"Hey, Dad, look. I found three new friends," yelled Victor from across the field.

Vinnie looked around and saw Victor in the middle of a group of chicks, spreading his wings and flapping them around vigorously. He managed to rise off the ground but then came crashing down, landing on his beak. Getting to his feet, Victor strutted around the group.

Vinnie saw his son rise into the air. Then his heart beat faster as he saw Victor crash to the ground and smash his beak. Alarmed, he rushed over to Victor. When he saw that he was unharmed, his concern turned to anger, and he began to beat Victor with his beak. He pushed him with his chest all the way back to the nest and then beat him more on the neck and head.

"You foolish child, don't you know that a chick is never to stray from the nest? The island is full of a million chicks, and if your mother and I cannot find you to feed, you will die."

Victor put his head down. "Father," he said, "I was so excited to find that I could move over the ground without touching it with my feet that I forgot the rule." He looked up at Vinnie, expecting him to be happy with his new skill. Instead Vinnie again beat him on the neck with his beak, still angry about not finding his son near the nest.

In the hope of finding something to please his father, Victor puffed up his chest and asked, "Did you see my new friends? We were playing 'Can you do this?' I am the only one that can fly, or at least get my feet off the ground."

Vinnie began to relax. He knew that he should encourage his son to develop survival skills. He allowed his son to peck at his beak and be fed. He was pleased to see Victor's greediness. Victor was growing into a strong bird. When Hester came back from the sea with more food, she, too, approached the nest as if that is where she expected him to be. Vinnie did not say anything to her about finding Victor missing.

A few days later, when Vinnie came to the nest from the sea, Victor did not beg to be fed. This was so unusual for this chick that Vinnie waited near the nest for the begging to begin. When it did not, he approached his son and asked, "Are you feeling all right, son?"

At first Victor did not respond. Then, somberly he said, "Dad, one of my friends has not eaten in four days now. His parents have not returned from the sea."

Vinnie looked around and saw, across the field, one chick lying in his nest with his head over the side. There was no adult bird in the area. As he looked up, he saw the carcass of an adult bird caught in the branches of an ironwood tree. Unable to free himself, he had perished.

"I am not very hungry," said Victor. "Could you give my share to my friend Chester today?"

Without any hesitation Vinnie answered firmly, "No, we must not interfere with the way it is."

"Father, he is so hungry, and I have so much. Can't we give him just a little bit?"

"I would spill my food on the ground before I would feed this chick," said Vinnie. "Without two parents to bring a chick to full growth, he would die. Better that it be now. That is the way it is."

Victor put his head down and would not beg. Vinnie flew away and did not return for several days.

When Vinnie returned, Chester was dead, and Victor begged for food without a word.

At another time, Victor watched one nearby chick coughing and vomiting. A fishing line hung from his beak and had become tangled around his leg. It dangled around him as he walked. A few days later, the chick began to limp as the line tightened around his leg, cutting off the circulation.

One day, when the chick was struggling to walk, the leg folded under him where the line was attached. He never walked again, and soon the parents did not return to the nest to feed him.

Victor saw how hungry and thin his friend was becoming, but he said nothing to his parents about sharing. One day the chick did not raise his head. Victor knew about death now. He repeated to himself, "This is the way it is."

One day Victor flapped his wings, and his body rose high off the ground. He saw the sea over the sand hill. He saw hundreds of nests with chicks on or near them. He was so excited as he flew farther and farther that he did not realize how far he had come. When he crash-landed, he was near a nest he had never seen before. Victor walked without direction, seeing nothing familiar.

Victor thought, "How am I to find my nest? Am I to die because my parents cannot find me to feed me?" The phrase "this is the way it is" kept running through his head.

Victor's steps became faster and faster. He kept looking around to see if could find anything familiar, even the dreaded ironwood tree. He saw none of his friends. Other parents ignored him. He knew he could expect no help from any quarter. He was lost.

The sun dipped over the horizon as a dark chill crept into the air. Fear gripped Victor as he began to stumble. His legs were rubbery underneath him, and he did not trust himself to fly. He was afraid his father would beat him and yet more afraid that no one would care enough to beat him, out here and alone through the night. Victor was alone in the dark for the first time in his life.

Salt and moisture dripped from his eyes and ran down the grooves on his beak, dropping to the ground. He was too frightened to know how tired he was. After what seemed like hours, he heard a familiar sound; it was his mother calling his name. Victor jumped up and made all the noises he knew how to make. Hester's voice grew closer. Soon she was standing before him. He expected to get beaten by her beak and chest, but she rushed up to him and put her neck around his. Silently she led him back to their nest. Vinnie was pretending to sleep, but Victor heard a sigh of relief coming from his father a short time later. Victor was happy to be home and vowed to be more careful in the future He knew the way it was.

CHAPTER 10

The Sharks

• • •

SEVERAL WEEKS LATER VICTOR GAZED out at the sea before him with growing excitement. Out there was the future—an unknown world. He pranced
back and forth on the beach. He spread his wings and flapped them. They
reached out far on either side of him, and when he leaned one way or the
other, the tip of a wing would dip into the sand. He practiced running for
a few steps with his wings outstretched. The cool wind beneath his wings
felt good in the warm afternoon sun.

As he ran and flapped, Victor was startled to find himself airborne.
When he tired quickly, he stopped flapping and yet found that he continued
to rise in the air with a warm flow of air beneath him. He looked down and
saw the island off to his right, so he leaned to his right and his body followed
him. Victor was heading back to the island, but was coming closer to the
water. He flapped with short excursions but did not gain much height in the
air. Perhaps he would not make it back to the land. How angry his father
would be to find him out at sea, yet how would his father even think to look
for him here? His heart beat fast, and he began to pant.

As he looked down and saw several large fish circling the area, he felt
a chill go through him.

Could these be the sharks he had heard about? Fear gave him extra strength, and with the last of his energy, he aimed for the sand dune and crashed into it. He lay still for a long time until he summoned the will to return home. He waited for his parents to return.

When Hester landed in front of his nest and waddled over to stand before him, Victor noted for the first time that he had to bend over to receive food from his mother. He was growing fast and was now larger than his mother. Both of his parents had to work hard to keep him from being hungry these past few days.

Victor looked around and saw that the other chicks were also growing larger than their parents.

He also realized that there was no food on the island and that parents had to fish at sea to feed the chicks.

Victor turned to his father. "You are wearing yourselves out getting food for me.

I should be able to do that for myself, don't you think?"

Vinnie was pleased that Victor was so wise for his young age. Vinnie stood next to the nest and said, "Soon now all of these parents will cease to come back to the nests they have tended for these long months."

Victor's eyes widened as he remembered those large fish circling the island. How could he fly over the sea to fish?

"What will happen to all of those chicks that have never strayed more than twenty feet from their nests since they were born? What will they do?"

Vinnie looked pensively out over the sea. "Victor, they will either fly and leave this island, or they will starve on it."

"Do you mean to say that someday the parents will just fly off and never come back?"

"That is exactly what I mean. This will happen very soon now," said Vinnie.

"What about all those big fish out there circling the island? What about them?" asked Victor.

"How do you know about the sharks?"

"I saw them," admitted Victor. "I flew away from the island and saw them below."

Vinnie looked away and stood next to his son for a long time saying nothing. Victor wanted his father to say something, even get angry.

"Are you angry with me, father?"

Vinnie just leaned over to peck a sand speck from Victor's neck. "It is time," Vinnie said as he walked away.

Victor did not know what to make of his father's response until his mother did not return to feed him. He remembered his father's words: "Someday soon, the chicks will either have to fly off the island to find their own food or starve to death on the island."

There were fewer and fewer adult birds coming back to the nest, and the chicks were getting restless. They were forming groups along the sand dunes. Some were running and flapping, some taking off into the air. Victor remembered the great fish circling the island and how tired he had become when he flew out over the sea, yet it was time to get ready to leave this life as he knew it.

Stretching his big wings out again and again, Victor flapped vigorously. He ran down the sand and flapped until he was in the air. He circled, landed, and rose into the air. He practiced taking off and landing for two days. By the second day, Victor was hungry. The exercise he was getting was making him hungrier than he could ever remember. Growling in his stomach woke him up that night.

When the sun rose, Victor knew that he must leave the island or die of starvation. He walked over to the sand hill and ran down the beach, launching himself into the air.

Hester and Vinnie had flown to the highest sand hill and stood watching.

"There he is," said Hester to Vinnie. "He looks so strong and yet so young."

They watched Victor run down the dune and take flight over the lagoon until he was out of sight.

Just as they were about to leave, they saw Victor returning to the island carrying a big fish in his beak. He landed and dropped the fish in front of a group of his friends Victor then spread his wings and flapped them. The other chicks did the same. He ran down the dunes with his wings outstretched.

One by one some other chicks followed him. He took to the air and circled over the water a short way.

"Look," said Hester. "Victor is helping his friends to survive. He is teaching them to practice before they fly out too far and can't get back."

"That does look like what he is doing," Vinnie said. "By doing that teaching, he is getting stronger himself. I am proud of our son; we both did a good job, Hester."

As some young birds spread their wings, the wings did not stretch all the way out. They drooped in the middle.

"Look over there, Hester," Vinnie said. "That chick spread his wings, and they did not unfold, but drooped. As hard as he tries to fly, he will not be able to. This chick will never leave the island. In a few days, he will be dead."

"Oh dear," said Hester. "Those parents spent so many months birthing and feeding that chick. What a waste. I hope they do not have to watch this."

"Look at that chick over there," Vinnie noted. "He came back to the island and landed with a thud. Looks like he has broken his wing." The chick did not move.

Another chick who had run down the hill and launched into the air got frightened and turned around to get back to land, but he couldn't stay in the air. He dropped down at the water's edge.

Immediately, a shark fin broke the water, and the chick disappeared. The water changed color where the chick had floated. Groups of sharks circled, waiting for another chick to drop from the sky. For every ten chicks that rose into the air on that day, one was eaten by sharks.

Later in the afternoon, Victor headed out to sea. He circled the island and then headed over the lagoon. Hester stood on her toes trying to see the last of their chick. Victor disappeared from view.

Vinnie whispered to himself, "May the world be kind to you, great heart, you beautiful and gifted freak of nature."

Hester and Vinnie went their separate ways with the full knowledge that they would meet again here on this spot the following year to raise a chick of their own. They knew that they were mates for life and that they were successful nest builders. Life was good, and Hester and Vinnie were happy.

Both were free to fly with the wind, eat from whatever part of the sea they chose, and know that they would return to the island to be together in another season. And that is the way it is.

THE END

Postscript

• • •

In 2006 the World Conservation Union listed the Laysan albatross as vulnerable to extinction. Ten percent are killed by long fishing lines dragged behind barges. Another ten percent die by ingesting the increasing plastic and garbage they perceive as food. Each year a full 5 tons of plastics are brought back by the parents and fed to their chicks. Some chicks cannot fly and die on the island, some are eaten by sharks when they fledge, or drown at sea.

Ocean front countries discharge into the sea, barges, fishing factories, cruise ships, pleasure yachts and sailboats toss plastic and garbage overboard while at sea, thinking with an "out of sight, out of mind" mentality. One late night on a recent cruise ship voyage, I personally witnessed men opening the cargo door on a deck below, and spend the next hour tossing large garbage bags into the sea. This must save a lot of money over disposal fees, but multiplied many times over on a daily basis year in and year out, could explain the sea of garbage washing up every year on the Island of Midway which is 2,000 miles from anywhere. When plastic degrades, it does not disappear, but grinds down to smaller particles that are perceived as food by fish and sea creatures. It makes one wonder why a score of whales or dolphins would beach themselves to die.

If any readers have comments, or more to the point solutions or ideas to diminish the sea of garbage, the flaking lead from remaining military buildings, and the tons of plastic that are degrading this wildlife, contact me at rdidomen@gmail.com.
Ruth DiDomenico

References

• • •

Google "Midway Islands"

Google "Laysan albatross"